A Friendship JOURNAL

For personal notes & mementos
with quotes & illustrations

Edited by Evelyn L. Beilenson
Designed by Michel Design

PETER PAUPER PRESS, INC.
WHITE PLAINS · NEW YORK

For John Beilenson

Copyright © 1990
Peter Pauper Press, Inc.
202 Mamaroneck Avenue
White Plains, NY 10601
ISBN 0-88088-703-6
Printed in Hong Kong

Dear Diary . .

A journal or diary (the French call it a *journal intime*) is a written account of the day's happenings and reflections. The author keeps this record for a number of reasons.

A nne Frank, one of the 20th Century's best-known diarists, enduring the unendurable, noted in her journal that "I can write down my thoughts and feelings, otherwise I would be absolutely stifled." Virginia Woolf realized that if you don't write down the events of the day, they've "gone down the sink to oblivion." Oscar Wilde amusingly writes in *The Importance of Being Earnest*, that "I never travel without my diary. One should always have something sensational to read on the train."

M ost journals will never be published, however, but are for personal use and enjoyment. *Your* diary may be your best friend, or sometimes even your enemy. Whichever, and for whatever reason, turn the page. write on, and enjoy!

E.L.B.

This day and your life, my friend, are God's
gifts to you—so give thanks and be joyful always!

Jim Beggs

Friend is a word of Royal tone
Friend is a Poem all alone.

A Persian Poet

Be slow in choosing a friend, slower in changing.
Benjamin Franklin

_____

_____

_____

_____

_____

_____

_____

_____

_____

_____

_____

_____

_____

_____

_____

_____

_____

_____

_____

_____

_____

_____

_____

Who ceases to be a friend, never was one.

Anonymous

*Before you put on a frown, my friend, make
absolutely certain there are no smiles available.*

Jim Beggs

A friend to all is a friend to none.

Aristotle

Every man should have a fair sized cemetery
in which to bury the faults of his friends.

Henry Brooks Adams

Be not the fourth friend of him who had
three before and lost them.

John Casper Lavater

True happiness consists not in the multitude
of friends, but in their worth and choice.

Ben Jonson

"Stay" is a charming word in a friend's vocabulary.

Amos Bronson Alcott

To find fulfillment, my friend, don't coexist
with life—embrace it!

Jim Beggs

_____

_____

_____

_____

_____

_____

_____

_____

_____

_____

_____

_____

_____

_____

_____

_____

_____

_____

_____

_____

_____

_____

_____

_____

*A friend is a person with whom I may be
sincere. Before him, I may think aloud.*

Ralph Waldo Emerson

A man's friendships are one of the best measures of his worth.

Charles Darwin

*Friendship is a word the very sight of which
in print makes the heart warm.*

Augustine Birrell

_____

_____

_____

_____

_____

_____

_____

_____

_____

_____

_____

_____

_____

_____

_____

_____

_____

_____

_____

_____

_____

_____

_____

_____

_____

_____

What we say is important, my friend, for in most cases the mouth speaks what the heart is full of.

Jim Beggs

_____

_____

_____

_____

_____

_____

_____

_____

_____

_____

_____

_____

_____

_____

_____

_____

_____

_____

_____

_____

_____

_____

The only rose without thorns is friendship.

Madeleine de Scudéry

We are advertis'd by our loving friends.
William Shakespeare

When my friends are one-eyed, I look at their profile.

Joseph Joubert

A friend is a present you give yourself.

Robert Louis Stevenson

*The only reward of virtue is virtue; the only
way to have a friend is to be one.*

Ralph Waldo Emerson

*Of what shall a man be proud, if he is not
proud of his friends?*

Robert Louis Stevenson

If a man has a friend, what need has he of medicines?

Bhartrihari

When friends ask, there is no tomorrow.

Proverb

The ornament of a house is the friends who frequent it.

Ralph Waldo Emerson

A faithful friend is a true image of the Deity.

Napoleon Bonaparte

Choose thy friends like thy books, few but choice.

James Howell

Friends are like melons; shall I tell you why?
To find one good you must a hundred try.

Claude Mermet

Laughter is not a bad beginning for a
friendship, and it is the best ending for one.

Oscar Wilde

_____

_____

_____

_____

_____

_____

_____

_____

_____

_____

_____

_____

_____

_____

_____

_____

_____

_____

_____

_____

_____

_____

_____

_____

A real friend is one who walks in when the
rest of the world walks out.

Walter Winchell

Judge not thy friend until thou standest in his place.

Rabbi Hillel

_A friend you have to buy won't be worth
what you pay for him._

G. D. Prentice

The greatest healing therapy is friendship and love.
Hubert Humphrey

In prosperity our friends know us; in
adversity we know our friends.

John Churton Collins

_____

_____

_____

_____

_____

_____

_____

_____

_____

_____

_____

_____

_____

_____

_____

_____

_____

_____

_____

_____

_____

What is a friend? A single soul dwelling in two bodies.

Aristotle

*You can choose your friends but you can't
choose your relatives.*

Charlie Brown

_____

_____

_____

_____

_____

_____

_____

_____

_____

_____

_____

_____

_____

_____

_____

_____

_____

_____

_____

_____

_____

_____

_____

A friend in need is a friend indeed.

English Proverb

There are three faithful friends—an old wife,
an old dog, and ready money.

Benjamin Franklin

Friendship is like money, easier made than kept.

Samuel Butler

_____

_____

_____

_____

_____

_____

_____

_____

_____

_____

_____

_____

_____

_____

_____

_____

_____

_____

_____

_____

_____

_____

_____

_____

Friends are needed both for joy and for sorrow.

Yiddish Proverb

One who looks for a friend without faults will have none.

Hasidic Saying

*Friendship is the only cement that will ever
hold the world together.*

Woodrow Wilson

_____

_____

_____

_____

_____

_____

_____

_____

_____

_____

_____

_____

_____

_____

_____

_____

_____

_____

_____

_____

_____

_____

A man, Sir, should keep his friendships in constant repair.

Samuel Johnson

Hold a true friend with both hands.

Nigerian Proverb

Of course platonic friendship is possible—but only between husband and wife.

Anonymous

A home-made friend wears longer than one
you buy in the market.

Austin O'Malley

Friends should be preferred to kings.

Voltaire

_____

_____

_____

_____

_____

_____

_____

_____

_____

_____

_____

_____

_____

_____

_____

_____

_____

_____

_____

_____

_____

*I always felt that the great high privilege,
relief and comfort of friendship was that one
had to explain nothing.*

Katherine Mansfield